TIME MANAGEMENT MASTERY

TIME MANAGEMENT MASTERY

Maximizing Productivity

JIM STEPHENS

QuantumQuill Press

CONTENTS

Introduction

In summary, the critical need to manage time in the workforce is directly impacted by the effectiveness of work in individual time management skills. As a function of job satisfaction and success, the majority of job holders in the U.S. perform work that is unsatisfactory resulting in what would seem like at first glance a premature end to jobs. This study attempts to measure time management skills and provide a quantitative assessment to better equip business and industry service industries to assist time mismanagement. Further research would be helpful to determine if non-traditional students and traditional students across both genders, majors, and classifications of student substantial differences exist in time management skills.

In the work domain, effective time management skills are a key career success factor. Person-job fit metrics incorporate time management proficiency as a core part because of its substantial impact on work behavior, work productivity, and job satisfaction. Time mismanagement tends to result in lost time and significantly less success. By exploring if hypothetical differences can be found in non-traditional students and traditional students in college, organizations can explain if differences exist. By uncovering the differences, service industries will be better able to provide appropriate time mismanagement training to serve a significant subgroup of working Americans.

CHAPTER 1

Understanding Time Management

Many college instructors who are very strong 'time managers' may not have intended to, nor understand why, this particular label applies to them. You may have a very clear understanding of the difference in your own personal goals and priorities. You may strictly set and follow your personal standards for quality and time commitment related to your job. You may also have a very deep understanding of your core values and this understanding is the driving force behind your ability to manage your time and productivity efficiently, effectively, and ethically. Understanding how to better develop your own personal understanding of management principles will provide you the foundation to better teach them. Beginning to comprehend the nature of the principles of management will improve your own personal outcomes. As your tenure in the profession continues, understanding these principles will continue to improve your own understanding of your personal goals. Convert your new self-knowledge into a springboard for better understanding and teaching these principles. Explore how these principles translate effectively into effective teaching.

How many times have you heard or experienced a workshop where the speaker says that if you can effectively plan, organize, direct and control your personnel and assets, you have experience with the principles of good management? Doesn't that seem easy? So, if you understand the principles of management, why don't they always transfer well into the classroom? Instructors often offer a number of reasons for the difficulty these principles have in transferring over to teaching. First, many instructors lack formal training in education and management. Second, many teachers got into education because they enjoy working with young people, not because they want to oversee teams of people. Understanding the basic idea that time management is really about managing individuals and not minutes scheduled on a daily plan is the next step you will take on your path to effective management of this important asset.

Why don't management concepts always transfer well to classrooms?

2.1. Importance of Time Management

Managing time effectively and the perception of time affects personal productivity and stress. Feeling time in this manner specifically accentuates the role of time, as suggested. It is more quotidian in the relation of temporal specificity intriguingly stressed regarding the 'impossibility' when thinking of future events or this feeling can differentiate the participants good and poor in managing time. If so, this relationship and potentially why, this is where future work can start moving beyond general descriptions and measurements of time project specificity. In addition, as proposed, choice can enhance this effect. Notably, individuals are even more affected by time and money.

2.1. Importance of time management. It is quite cliché but worth mentioning that "time is gold." We need to understand that time is a limited and non-renewing resource. Once we have wasted it, we can never take it back. That is why it is very important to manage and use our time effectively. The ideal is to be able to maximize the use of our time without getting stressed out or burned out. By focusing one's attention on the highest-priority tasks that have the greatest impact, the law of cause and effect is brought into play. The time and energy expended support that activity and the ultimate payoff is multiplied several times over. An example of this is an employee who is an excellent technician (that's the effect), has leadership on the job, is a team player, can manage his resources and has a never-say-die attitude and initiative (that's the cause). If an employee always performs at this level, sooner or later, he will be promoted to a higher position or even given an award.

2.2. Common Time Management Challenges

Being goal oriented. Sometimes, people experience that they don't necessarily have an issue with how they manage their time, but perhaps they have goals that aren't very clear. It's hard to manage your time effectively when you lack focus in terms of your direction. Most time management processes include a step at the beginning where you identify what your objectives are. By setting good, clear objectives that can then be translated to daily, step by step activities, you have a clear road map. These goals can then be broken down into step by step tasks. No time to plan. Many people share that they would like to effectively manage their time better, but they say they just don't have time to set objectives and plan for those objectives. It's wise and easy to fall into a reactionary mode of operation, putting out fires and working on tasks that are urgent, however likely aren't important. By setting aside the time to plan, we can be in a proactive/strategic mode of operating instead of a reactionary in a reactionary/urgent mode of operation.

A list of common time management challenges includes: interruptions. One of the most common things people express frustration over when it comes to time management is their ability to get interrupted. Whether they're trying to work on a project and a co-worker comes over to talk or they are working on a report and their boss needs them to do something else right then, interruptions make it hard to manage our time effectively. Too many priorities. With the increased workload that most of us have, juggling multiple projects at once is simply something most people experience on a regular basis. Although it is frustrating to experience this, learning some tools to help manage those times when you can't avoid multiple demands will be helpful.

CHAPTER 2

Strategies for Effective Time Management

• Gain control by building a routine and establishing habits. According to some reports, close to 40% of the daily actions are automated, which means that the brain doesn't need to constantly engage; it doesn't put pressure to make decisions. For optimal time management, creating habits that are constructed from a routine helps the brain focus on getting the most important tasks done. People cannot change their daily routine through willpower alone. They must build an automated action that occurs consistently with a cue. Develop a good habit by building them around cues. Making a cup of coffee can be a cue to start writing, brushing teeth can be a cue to start exercising, and so on. Researchers also relate cues to the joy of performance (mesolimbic pathway), which causes motivation and rewards the brain when the cue occurs. So, by associating an action with a cue multiple times, the brain craves the cue, thus developing a habitual response.

Strategies for effective time management. Once you begin to take control of your time and find ways to fit all the activities and priorities into your life, you will be surprised by how creative you can be and how efficient you can become. It sometimes feels like there are not enough hours in the day to accomplish everything on your to-do list. A good time management system is proven to help you effectively accomplish your work without the needlessly high levels of stress and fatigue. To make this happen, try some of these strategies for better time management:

3.1. Setting Clear Goals and Priorities

When considering this in terms of results, I find that setting clear goals and priorities really helps and enables me to take a task and make it critical or trivial accordingly. When everything we do is made critical, critics are worthless. Focusing on a few tasks is the only way it is possible at all. The only thing you need to do is to watch those tasks, see them done, and enjoy adding up. The more you focus on the most important tasks, the shorter your time limit is to achieve them.

One tool that I found incredibly helpful is having clear goals. Knowing what is important and knowing your end goal enables me to easily discard easy tasks and spend time working on the hard ones because I have the confidence that it is contributing to my end goal. The ability to focus on the highest payoff activities pares down the immensely disparate creation of ideas and focuses on what is really important. I need to be smart enough to not see everything as of equal importance – it does not matter how fast I do many small tasks because, in the end, how much I managed to deliver is measured by the big important custom tasks.

Early in my working life, I always had a feeling that I did quite a lot, given the limited hours I had each day. The problem was that I was spending long hours working every day because I did not do things that contributed significantly to my end goal. It felt stressful and not feasible if I were to start working on a long-term project then juggle everything else at the same time.

3.2. Creating a Time Management Plan

By analyzing the varying levels of time management success that we demonstrate largely unconsciously at any given time, the analyst learns to track the very activities that the analyst him- or herself performs with an eye to results and according to focus, rather than to the mere activity of performing them. It goes without saying that all the important elements of a successful habits-based change are present in this approach. First and foremost is the discovery of the potential impact of improvements, followed by the decision-making and striving for the changes as much as possible. This awareness-based method precludes an external trainer imposing change upon the trainee. In all reality, through the methods learned, the driving force and takeaway from this life is that the individual being trained is, in fact, now the internal trainer who leads the charge for self-change.

One of the most valuable habits to build using the skills and mindfulness approach is the habit of using a time tracker. By keeping track of the activities that we are engaged in over time, we can get a realistic profile of how we manage our professional and personal duties. We inherently become aware of what we are doing, the choices we are making, and the prioritizations we are exercising. The resulting analysis allows us to see areas of improvement and, most importantly, to also remember the eight decision strategies in order to come up with real plans to actually improve our personal effectiveness.

1. Keeping track of how you manage your time systems currently. 2. Setting your time management goals. 3. Defining

your activities. 4. Designing the plan to align activities with goals. 5. Evaluating the improvement.

As discussed before, time management is primarily about intention, awareness, and decision. With that in mind, creating a successful time management plan entails five steps. These are:

3.3. Eliminating Time Wasters

Dealing with other people can be a professional time waster, and preventing this from happening is a fundamental skill in time management. There are, however, a number of different ways to do this. First, you should do everything you can to ensure "communication stays open." When you return phone calls, respond to an email, or follow up on important information, you should do so before the close of business each day. Alternatively, leaving important issues until the last minute can cause the situation to snowball. Call and respond to people who may have been offended by your delay or who may be angry with you before rumors start to fly. Don't allow meetings to escalate into shouting matches. Find someone who can help you manage the meeting, cutting through rhetoric and hyperbole, and help reach a sensible conclusion at the end. Finally, understand that there are some people you will not be able to work things out with. If this is the case, assure that they are not ruling your day at their convenience.

INTERPERSONAL PROBLEMS

A key element of time management is the ability to quickly and effectively eliminate time wasters from the work day. These "time wasters" are things that waste time during your work day and make it harder for you to manage your time effectively. Most workers cite meetings as their #1 time waster, but meetings are only that - a matter of cited perception. In truth, there are a number of different time wasters. As a worker, it is important to "know your time wasters" so that you can identify and eliminate them right from the start.

CHAPTER 3

Techniques to Boost Productivity

Take regular breaks. One of the most efficient time management techniques you can apply is to accomplish assignments in short, well-focused amounts of time, interplayed with regular rest pauses - 5 minutes every half an hour, for example. Breaks and headlines are very crucial. Operating at high rates for protracted periods tires you out. Analysis performed at difficult times in the mid-20th century in various fields such as assembly lines, armed conflict, and machinery-design laboratories attests to this. Minimizing exhaustion, on the other hand, means that not only can you maintain a healthy pace, but with correct planning, you can sustain it throughout the day. In summary, taking a 5-minute rest breather every 25-30 minutes may enhance the efficiency of the work and help avoid maladies such as RSI, carpal tunnel syndrome, and eye-ache.

Set timers for multiple jobs. You will often combine a series of short tasks into a 15-30 minute block. You cannot afford to lose track of time. A PC reminder that pops up on your screen can signal the change in task. In this way, you can keep track of your tasks. You can engage yourself to do things when your mind is switched on to a particular prompt. Short, targeted tasks put your brain on track and make you productive for the next job.

Techniques to boost productivity:

4.1. Prioritization Techniques

The PDCA Method: Propose a solution to the problem, develop and prepare a plan to implement the necessary change. Implement the plan, control the new process, measure its performance and make required adjustments until the desired results have been reached. If a new problem arises, solve it in the same way and make sure to document any changes made. Always be looking to make a task more efficient. Keep these steps in mind next time you run into a problem. You will be able to look at it in a more systematic manner in order to find the best solution. Also, it allows to solve the issue in an organized way, minimizing trial and error as you try to adjust and make things work. Not only does it provide a foundational perspective, but it also acts as a budget in times of scarce resources (time, money, etc.).

The ABC Method - If you have a big task, break it down by steps and title each step from A - to Do Now, B - to Do Next, and C - to Do Soon at the end. If you have trouble getting started, ask yourself which is the smallest part of this project that is essential to start right now. Once you start, you can pause to prioritize the C or the B and keep going. This is a great approach for the tasks you have been dragging for days or weeks. Just dive in, write down the steps, and progress with the A's. If something pops up and it is more important than the B-C steps that are left, pause and deal with it.

4.2. Time Blocking

Group time blocks in your daily schedule can be typically summarized as high-priority day-related batches, such as the following:

starting with early AM - exercise, fun, or time to relax; productivity warm-up; deep work on the most important tasks; daily check-ins and/or summary outputs; and cap triumphant wins and/or cap close of day. Allocate a time block for reviewing the daily task list, next day task planning, and partially completing any administrative tasks that are not that important. With a little bit of key organization, time blocking can then be combined to achieve high productivity each day. Over time, practicing daily time blocking can be linked to weekly planning sessions and monthly or even annual planning, although these might be at lower levels of scheduling detail-task focus. Just like owning a hammer won't make you into a great carpenter, to become productive, there is a mindset and method shift that is essential to consider when implementing time blocking.

Time blocking simply refers to the process of setting up specific blocks in your calendar for a specific purpose. For example, time blocks set aside for producing reports to management, planning for the company town hall, preparing the implementation plan, or even conducting the company's strategic planning exercise. Therefore, time blocking simply refers to blocking out a specific length of time to work on an important task. Similar to many successful productivity systems, time blocking works extremely well because it makes it real and specific. Instead of having a vague 2-hour block to do important work, time blocking tells you exactly what needs to be done during those 2 hours - the start times, the end times, and even the intermediate steps to be taken so that the said task can be considered as done or completed. Time blocking ensures you stick to your time by holding you accountable to the stuff you scheduled. In addition, it also makes you respect your own time as you now schedule your life instead of trying to fit it into the leftover time.

4.3. Pomodoro Technique

The Pomodoro Technique helps you power through distractions, hyperfocus, and get things done in short bursts. It creates a sense of urgency. It is a good technique for people who have trouble focusing when time managing. The best part about the Pomodoro Technique is that it is free to use and very simple to do. After all, it is not a software, nor are you required to participate in any membership. The best of all, it can be used by everybody because it is very easy to understand.

The Pomodoro Technique is a simple time-management method created by Francesco Cirillo in the 1980s. The technique is based on intervals of 25 minutes (so-called "pomodoros") split by short breaks. One hour is divided into four 25-minute pomodoros followed by a break. Each 25 minutes of concentrated work is called a "pomodoro". The pomodoros could come in short strings of work followed by short breaks and, what Francesco specifically emphasizes as fundamental, long breaks. He uses a kitchen timer shaped like a tomato (in Italian "pomodoro"), so the technique was named after that.